MW01002365

PHOTO HERE

NAME: _____

ADDRESS: _____

_____

PHONE NUMBER: _____

SIGNATURE: _____

Greetings, fellow traveler!

You are now the owner of your very own California Missions Passport and have taken the first step into the historical adventure of a lifetime!

Why take such a journey? You get to follow the bells of the El Camino Real—the road which lead to all 21 missions; ride along the Pacific Coast Highway; explore the four Spanish presidios which once housed many Spanish soldiers; venture through hills, valleys, and open plains; walk through historical towns, see the swallows of Mission San Juan Capistrano, the wooden bells of Mission San Buenaventura, the rooms where Saint Junipero Serra resided in Mission San Carlos Borromeo de Carmelo, and so much more!

To record your journey, every time you visit a California mission you must place a STAMP, STICKER, or PHOTO inside the box associated to its respective mission. Once you finish the passport you would have completed the California Mission Challenge! Good luck and safe travels!

-D. Alexander

The California Missions

The Spanish missions in California are 21 religious settlements; established by Catholic Franciscan priests between 1769 and 1833, to expand Catholicism among the Native Americans in what is today the state of California. The missions were a way for the Spanish Empire to colonize the most northern and western parts of Spain's North American territory. The missionaries introduced European fruits, vegetables, cattle, horses, ranching and technology all throughout Alta California. However, the missions also brought serious negative reactions and consequences to the Native American populations with whom the Spaniards came in contact with.

Mexico achieved independence in 1821, taking Alta California along with it, but the missions maintained authority over native neophytes and control of vast land until the government secularized the missions in 1833. This took away the Catholic Church's control over the mission system, thus dividing the mission lands into many of the Ranchos of California.

Despite the fact that the original reason for the Spanish mission system no longer survives, many of California's missions are still active religious, educational, and historical centers of the surrounding communities. The impact the mission system has had on California culture, economics, and history can still be felt to this day. Today, the surviving mission buildings are the state's oldest structures and are the most-visited historic monuments.

Junípero Serra (November 24, 1713 – August 28, 1784) was a Roman Catholic Spanish priest of the Franciscan Order who founded the first nine of 21 Spanish missions in California from San Diego to San Francisco, in what was then called Alta California. Serra was beatified by Pope John Paul II on September 25, 1988, in Vatican City and canonized by Pope Francis on September 23, 2015, at the Basilica of the National Shrine of the Immaculate Conception in Washington, D.C.

1   <u>The Mother of the Missions</u>

MISSION SAN DIEGO DE ALCALA

Established: July 16, 1769

Founder: Fr. Junipero Serra

10818 San Diego Mission Rd., San Diego, CA
92108

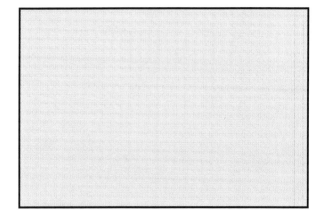

The Father of the Missions 2

MISSION SAN CARLOS
BORROMEO DEL RIO CARMELO

Established: June 3, 1770

Founder: Fr. Junipero Serra

3080 Rio Road Carmel, CA 93923

3 The Mission of the Sierras

MISSION SAN ANTONIO DE PADUA

Established: July 14, 1771

Founder: Fr. Junipero Serra

1 Mission Creek Road, Jolon, CA 93928

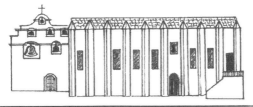

MISSION SAN GABRIEL ARCANGEL

Established: August 8, 1771

Founder: Fr. Pedro Cambon & Angel Somera

428 S. Mission Drive, San Gabriel, CA 91776

5 The Mission in the Valley of Bears

MISSION SAN LUIS OBISPO

Established: September 1, 1772

Founder: Fr. Junipero Serra

751 Palm Street, San Luis Obispo, CA 93401

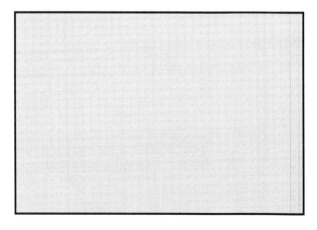

MISSION SAN FRANCISCO DE ASIS
(MISSION DOLORES)

Established: June 29, 1776

Founder: Fr. Francisco Palou & Pedro Benito Cambon

3321 Sixteen Street, San Francisco, CA 94114

7   The Jewel of the Missions

MISSION SAN JUAN CAPISTRANO

Established: November 1, 1776

Founder: Fr. Junipero Serra

26801 Ortega Hwy., San Juan Capistrano, CA 92675

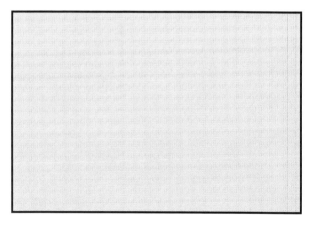

MISSION SANTA CLARA DE ASIS

Established: January 12, 1777

Founder: Fr. Junipero Serra

500 El Camino Real, Santa Clara, CA 95053

9   The Mission by the Sea

MISSION SAN BUENAVENTURA

Established: March 31, 1782

Founder: Fr. Fermin de Lausen

211 E. Main Street, Ventura, CA 93001

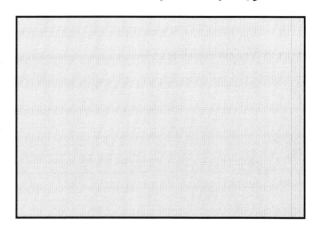

MISSION SANTA BARBARA

Established: December 4, 1786

Founder: Fr. Fermin de Lausen

2201 Laguna Street, Santa Barbara, CA 93105

MISSION LA PURISIMA

Established: December 8, 1787

Founder: Fr. Fermin de Lausen

2295 Purisima Road, Lompoc, CA 93436

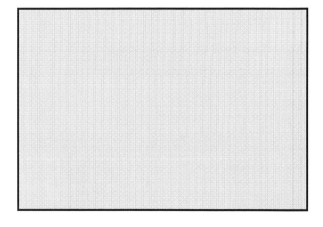

MISSION SANTA CRUZ

Established: August 28, 1791

Founder: Fr. Fermin de Lausen

130 Emmett Street, Santa Cruz, CA 95060

13

MISSION NUESTRA SENORA DE LA SOLEDAD

Established: October 9, 1791

Founder: Fr. Fermin de Lausen

36641 **Fort Romie Rd., Soledad, CA** 93960

MISSION SAN JOSE

Established: June 11, 1791

Founder: Fr. Fermin de Lausen

43300 Mission Blvd., Fremont, CA 94539

15 <u>The Mission of Music</u>

MISSION SAN JUAN BAUTISTA

Established: June 24, 1797

Founder: Fr. Fermin de Lausen

406 Second Street, San Juan Bautista, CA 95045

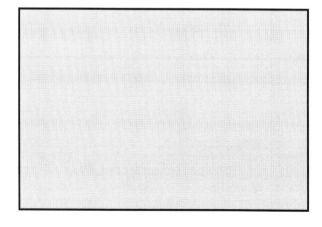

<u>The Mission on the Highway</u> 16

MISSION SAN MIGUEL ARCANGEL

Established: July 25, 1797

Founder: Fr. Fermin de Lausen

775 Mission Street, San Miguel, CA 93451

17   <u>The Mission of the Valley</u>

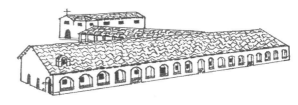

MISSION SAN FERNANDO REY

Established: September 8, 1797

Founder: Fr. Fermin de Lausen

15151 San Fernando Mission Blvd., Mission Hills, CA
91345

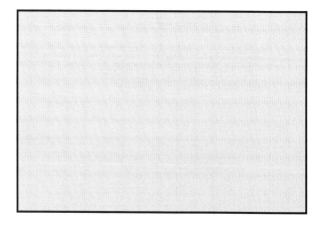

MISSION SAN LUIS REY

Established: June 13, 1798

Founder: Fr. Fermin de Lausen

4050 Mission Avenue, Oceanside, CA 92057

19

MISSION SANTA INES

Established: September 17, 1804

Founder: Fr. Estevan Tapis

1760 Mission Drive, Solvang, CA 93464

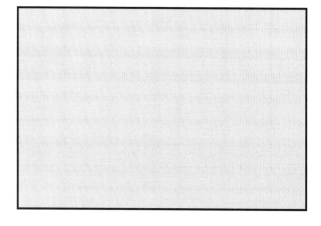

MISSION SAN RAFAEL ARCANGEL

Established: December 14, 1817

Founder: Fr. Vicente de Sarria

1104 Fifth Avenue, San Rafael, CA 94901

MISSION SAN FRANCISCO SOLANO

Established: July 4, 1823

Founder: Fr. Jose Altimira

114 East Spain Street, Sonoma, CA 95476

NOTES

NOTES

NOTES

Follow The Author!

Follow D. Alexander Ramirez on Facebook and find out what got him the idea of creating the *California Missions Passport*. Post your adventures and get updates on events and book signings.

CaliforniaMissionsPassport

Made in the USA
Las Vegas, NV
28 December 2020

14877875R00018